For Gilda with love,
L'Chiam!
— J. Marzollo

To my friends,
Matthew and Harrison
— J. Moffatt

Text copyright © 1997 by Jean Marzollo.
Illustrations copyright © 1997 by Judith Moffatt.

All rights reserved. Published by Scholastic Inc.
SCHOLASTIC, CARTWHEEL BOOKS, and associated logos
are trademarks and/or registered trademarks of Scholastic Inc.
Lexile is a registered trademark of MetaMetrics, Inc.

Library of Congress Cataloging-in-Publication Data is available.

ISBN-13: 978-0-590-84779-7
ISBN-10: 0-590-84779-1

20 19 18 17 16 15 14   10 11 12 13 14/0

Printed in the U.S.A. 40 • This edition first printing, June 2008

I'm a caterpillar

by Jean Marzollo
Illustrated by Judith Moffatt

Cartwheel
B·O·O·K·S ®

SCHOLASTIC INC.
New York   Toronto   London   Auckland   Sydney
Mexico City   New Delhi   Hong Kong   Buenos Aires

I'm a caterpillar.
Munch.
Crunch.

I'm getting bigger!
Munch.
Crunch.

Munch. Crunch.
Munch. Crunch.

That's it.
No more food.
I'm done.

It's time to hang from a stem.

I wait,
and wait,
and wait.

I shiver.
I twist.
I split my skin!

My old skin falls away.
I am soft inside.
I am a pupa (PEW-pah).

I grow a shell
to protect the pupa.
I am now a chrysalis
(KRIS-ah-lis).

I keep changing.
Soon I'll come out.
What will I be?

A butterfly!
Push.
Crack.
Wow!
I'm free!

My wings are all wet.

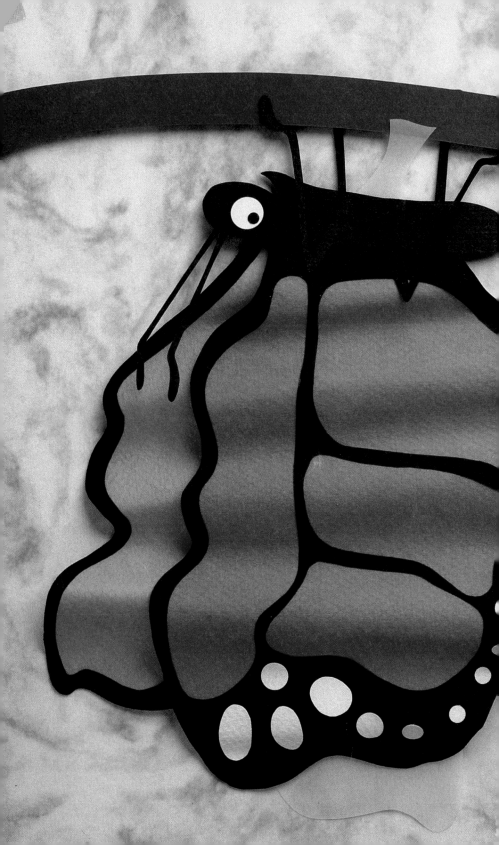

My wings dry off.
They unfold.

Flap. Flap.
Hey!
I can fly!
Ta-da!

I visit flowers.
I drink nectar.
Yum!

My mouth is like
a straw.
Sip.
Sip.
Sip.

I have a mate.
We visit many flowers.

We're not afraid of birds.
They know that
we taste awful.

Soon I will lay my eggs.

The eggs have thin shells.

Baby caterpillars crawl out.

Hi! I'm a caterpillar.

Munch. Crunch.

caterpillar

What will happen
to me next?
Do you know?

chrysalis

eggs

butterfly